Weekly Reader Children's Book Club presents
selections from

REVISITED

Favorites Old and New

By CHARLES M. SCHULZ

HOLT, RINEHART AND WINSTON
New York

FOR JOYCE

Copyright © 1955, 1956, 1957, 1958, 1959 by United Feature Syndicate, Inc.

All rights reserved, including the right to reproduce
this book or portions thereof in any form.

In Canada, Holt, Rinehart and Winston of Canada, Limited.

Library of Congress Catalog Card Number: 59-13405

ISBN: 0-03-029945-4

Printed in the United States of America

Weekly Reader Children's Book Club Edition

PEANUTS
REVISITED

I'VE LOST A LIBRARY BOOK..
YOU HAVE? OH, BOY! YOU'RE A DEAD DUCK!
COMIX

I'VE LOOKED ALL OVER, BUT I CAN'T FIND IT
I'D SAY YOU'RE A DEAD DUCK

I'VE LOOKED AND I'VE LOOKED AND I'VE LOOKED..
YOU KNOW WHAT, CHARLIE BROWN?

NO WHAT?
YOU'RE A DEAD DUCK!
SCHULZ

"LEARN TO READ," THEY SAY. "READING IS THE GREATEST THING IN THE WORLD!"

THEN THE NEXT THING YOU KNOW THEY WANT YOU TO TAKE BOOKS OUT FROM THE LIBRARY..

BUT, BOY, IF YOU LOSE ONE OF THEIR OL' BOOKS, THEN THEY WANNA KILL YOU!

I NEVER SAID I WANTED TO LEARN HOW TO READ!!!
SCHULZ

MAYBE THE LIBRARY THINKS YOU STOLE THEIR BOOK..

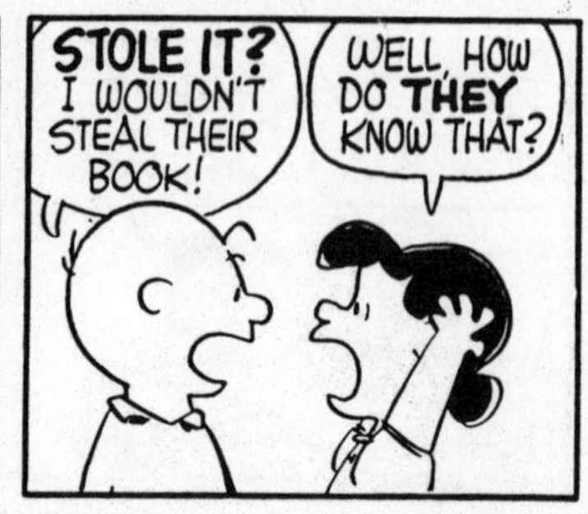
STOLE IT? I WOULDN'T STEAL THEIR BOOK!
WELL, HOW DO THEY KNOW THAT?

STOLE IT! GOOD GRIEF!
WELL, WHAT DO YOU EXPECT THEM TO THINK?

LIBRARIES ARE HUMAN, TOO, YOU KNOW!
SCHULZ

THIEF!
SCHULZ

LUCY SAYS YOU STOLE A LIBRARY BOOK, CHARLIE BROWN..

I DIDN'T STEAL THEIR BOOK!

YOU'RE SHOUTING, CHARLIE BROWN.. YOU DON'T HAVE TO SHOUT..
I'M SORRY.. I DIDN'T MEAN TO SHOUT... I..

DID YOU EVER SEE A THIEF WITH SUCH A ROUND HEAD?
SCHULZ

IF I DON'T FIND THAT LIBRARY BOOK, THEY'LL KILL ME!

SNOOPY, OL' PAL, YOU'RE THE ONLY ONE WHO SEEMS TO UNDERSTAND..

YOU'RE THE ONLY ONE I CAN TALK TO... YOU'RE THE ONLY..

Z

I THINK I'LL JUST CALL UP THE LIBRARY, AND TELL THEM I'VE LOST THEIR BOOK!

I THINK I'LL GO RIGHT OVER TO THE PHONE, AND CALL THEM UP!

I THINK I'LL JUST PICK UP THE PHONE, CALL THE LIBRARY AND TELL THEM THAT I'VE LOST THEIR BOOK..

I THINK I'LL DROP DEAD..
SCHULZ

LAST NIGHT I DREAMED THAT THE LIBRARY PEOPLE CAME TO GET ME..

THEY PUT BIG CHAINS ON ME, AND HIT ME OVER THE HEAD WITH BOOKS..THEN THE LIBRARY PEOPLE TURNED INTO THE F.B.I.

THEY KEPT CHASING ME OVER STATE LINES, AND THEN SOME CITIZEN GROUPS BEGAN TO THROW STONES AT ME..

I WAS SORT OF GLAD WHEN I WOKE UP!
SCHULZ

DID YOU EVER FIND YOUR LIBRARY BOOK, CHARLIE BROWN?

NO..
GEE, WHAT DO YOU THINK WILL HAPPEN?

WELL, I'LL TELL YOU...WHENEVER IT'S ONE MAN AGAINST AN INSTITUTION, THERE IS ALWAYS A TENDENCY FOR THE INSTITUTION TO WIN!

WHAT'S THE MATTER?
THE HEARING OF A GREAT TRUTH ALWAYS STUNS ME!
SCHULZ

DEAR LIBRARY, I HAVE LOST YOUR BOOK.

I CAN NOT FIND IT ANYWHERE.

I WILL COME TO THE LIBRARY AND TURN MYSELF IN.

PLEASE DO NOT HARM MY MOTHER AND FATHER.
SCHULZ

I FOUND IT

I FOUND MY LIBRARY BOOK! I LOOKED IN THE REFRIGERATOR AND THERE IT WAS! I FOUND IT!!!

I FOUND IT! I FOUND IT!! HA HA HA HA HA HA I FOUND IT! I FOUND IT! HEE HEE HEE HEE HEE I FOUND IT! I FOUND IT!!

IN ALL THIS WORLD THERE IS NOTHING MORE INSPIRING THAN THE SIGHT OF SOMEONE WHO HAS JUST BEEN TAKEN OFF THE HOOK!

WELL, I'LL BE!

I'VE BEEN AFRAID THIS WOULD HAPPEN SOME DAY... MOM!

I'VE SCRUBBED, AN' SCRUBBED, AN' SCRUBBED, BUT I CAN'T GET CLEAN..

I THINK I'VE REACHED THE 'POINT OF NO RETURN'!
SCHULZ

KLUNK!

KLUNK?!
SCHULZ

PEANUTS®
WHY CAN'T WE EVER WATCH WHAT I WANT TO WATCH?

I'M TIRED OF ALWAYS HAVING TO WATCH YOUR PROGRAMS!

IN FACT, I THINK I'LL CHANGE THE CHANNEL RIGHT NOW!

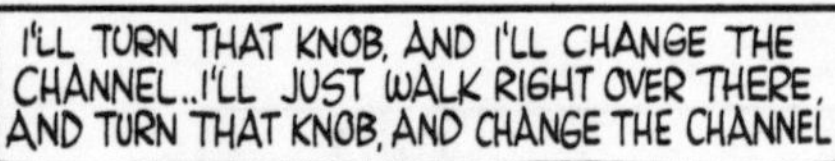
I'LL TURN THAT KNOB, AND I'LL CHANGE THE CHANNEL..I'LL JUST WALK RIGHT OVER THERE, AND TURN THAT KNOB, AND CHANGE THE CHANNEL

THAT'S JUST WHAT I THINK I'LL DO..I THINK I'LL WALK RIGHT OVER THERE, AND TURN THAT KNOB, AND CHANGE THAT CHANNEL...

I THINK I'LL WALK RIGHT OVER THERE, AND CHANGE THE CHANNEL...THAT'S JUST WHAT I'LL DO..I'LL WALK RIGHT OVER THERE, AND TURN THE KNOB...

SCHULZ
SIGH

PEANUTS

WHAM!

ONE PATCH OF ICE DOTH NOT A WINTER MAKE..
OH, SHUT UP!
SCHULZ

YOUR BLANKET?

I THINK MOMMY JUST WASHED IT, LINUS...I'LL BET IT'S HANGING OUT ON THE CLOTHESLINE..

SCHULZ

HEY, CHARLIE BROWN...DO YOU WANT ME TO FEED SNOOPY BEFORE WE GO?

SURE...HIS DOG FOOD IS RIGHT THERE IN THE CUPBOARD..

DID YOU PUT IT IN HIS DISH?
OF COURSE..

?
DOG FOOD
SCHULZ

PLUNK!

THUMP!

PLOP!

THERE ARE ALWAYS THOSE WHO NEVER QUITE MAKE IT..
SCHULZ

NOBODY LIKES ME...NOBODY!

HAVE YOU EVER STOPPED TO TRY TO FIGURE OUT WHY NOBODY LIKES YOU, CHARLIE BROWN?

OF COURSE I HAVE...AND I FOUND OUT WHY, TOO...

I'M UNPOPULAR!
SCHULZ

NOW, YOU KNOW WHAT YOU'RE GOING TO DO TOMORROW NIGHT, DON'T YOU?

SURE..I JUST GO UP TO THESE DIFFERENT HOUSES, RING THEIR DOORBELLS AND THEN SHOUT, "**TRICKS OR TREATS!**"

SAY, BY THE WAY... THERE'S NO LAW AGAINST THAT, IS THERE?
OF COURSE NOT..

I WOULDN'T WANT TO DO ANYTHING THAT MIGHT AROUSE THE F.B.I.!
SCHULZ

IS THAT YOU, LUCY?

UH, HUH...LINUS WILL BE ALONG IN A MINUTE...

HE WAS HAVING A LITTLE TROUBLE WITH HIS COSTUME..
?

HE'S NOT VERY GOOD YET WITH A SCISSORS!
SCHULZ

BOY, WHAT A DOPE HE TURNED OUT TO BE!

I TAKE HIM OUT FOR "TRICKS OR TREATS," AND HE GETS STAGE FRIGHT! HE JUST STOOD THERE!! HE WOULDN'T SAY A WORD!!!

SIGH

JUST WAIT 'TIL NEXT YEAR!!
SCHULZ

SCHULZ
INDECISION IS AN AWFUL THING..

PEANUTS
by
CHARLES M. SCHULZ
SIGH

GEE... I WISH I COULD GO TO SCHOOL..

I FEEL A NEED TO BE EDUCATED..

I WANT TO LEARN TO READ AND TO WRITE AND TO KNOW ALL ABOUT HISTORY..

I HAVE A RIGHT TO BE EDUCATED!

IN FACT, I DEMAND TO BE EDUCATED!!

KLUNK!

BOY, WILL VIOLET EVER BE SURPRISED..
PEANUTS
by
CHARLES M. SCHULZ

WHAT DO YOU HAVE THERE, CHARLIE BROWN?

THIS IS A PRESENT FOR VIOLET, BUT I'M SURE NOT GOING TO TELL YOU WHAT IT IS!

YOU THINK I'D TELL HER, DON'T YOU? OH, I'D NEVER DO THAT.. I PROMISE YOU.. I GIVE YOU MY SOLEMN PROMISE!

ALL RIGHT, THEN
LET YOU IN ON THE SECRET..IT'S A
ITTLE MUSIC BOX..
HEY, VIOLET! HE GOT YOU A MUSIC BOX!!

AAUGH!

NATURE IS A FASCINATING STUDY, LINUS...

NOW, TAKE THIS TREE.. SEE HOW THE BARK IS DAMAGED? IT ALMOST LOOKS LIKE SOMEONE HAS BEEN POUNDING HIS HEAD AGAINST IT...

MOST LIKELY, HOWEVER, IT WAS CAUSED BY A BEAR WHO MERELY STOPPED TO SHARPEN HIS CLAWS!

SIGH
WHAT IN THE WORLD WILL SHE BE LIKE WHEN SHE'S A TEEN-AGER?

I GUESS I COMPLAIN A LOT FOR NOTHING.. BEING A DOG REALLY ISN'T SO BAD...

BEEP!

EXCEPT FOR THE OCCASIONAL INDIGNITIES!
SCHULZ

BEEP!

SCHULZ

THERE'S ONE LITTLE FRAYED SPOT HERE.. ONE LITTLE PLACE...

RIGHT ALONG THE EDGE HERE.. I HAVE TO FIND... RIGHT ALONG HERE.. I HAVE TO... RIGHT ABOUT...

AH!

SCHULZ
SIGH..

SOMEBODY AT THE "SNICKER-SNACK" FACTORY SLIPPED UP..

THERE WAS SUPPOSED TO BE A MARBLE IN THIS BOX OF "SNICKER-SNACKS."..

LOOK WHAT HAPPENED..

FOUR HUNDRED MARBLES AND ONE 'SNICKER-SNACK'!
SCHULZ

"TO LIVE IS TO DANCE."

"TO DANCE IS TO LIVE!"
SCHULZ

MY DAD HATES ME!

WE WERE EATING SUPPER, AND I WAS FOOLING AROUND, AND HE SAID, "TRY TO ACT LIKE A HUMAN BEING."

THEN I SAID, "DEFINE 'HUMAN BEING.'"

MY DAD HATES ME!
SCHULZ

THERE SURE ARE A LOT OF THESE 'INSTANT' PRODUCTS ON THE MARKET

INSTANT COFFEE, INSTANT TEA, INSTANT PUDDING, INSTANT CEREAL

...INSTANT DISLIKE..
SCHULZ

"KINDERGARTEN.." LET'S SEE...

"A SCHOOL OR CLASS FOR YOUNG CHILDREN THAT DEVELOPS BASIC SKILLS AND SOCIAL BEHAVIOR BY GAMES., EXERCISES...

..AND SIMPLE HANDICRAFT."
SCHULZ

PEANUTS
NO!

YOU MUST THINK I'M CRAZY!

YOU SAY YOU'LL HOLD THE BALL, BUT YOU WON'T! YOU'LL PULL IT AWAY, AND I'LL BREAK MY NECK!
WHY, CHARLIE BROWN.. HOW YOU TALK...

I WOULDN'T THINK OF SUC A THING! I'M A CHANGE PERSON! LOOK...ISN'T THIS FACE YOU CAN TRUST?

ALL RIGHT...YOU HOLD THE BALL, AND I'LL COME RUNNING UP, AND KICK IT...

SHE DID IT AGAIN!!

WUMP!

SCHULZ
I ADMIRE YOU, CHARLIE BROWN... YOU HAVE SUCH FAITH IN HUMAN NATURE..

PEANUTS
WHAT ARE YOU MAKING?
THESE ARE SNOW-BUNNIES

CAN I HELP YOU, LUCY?

NO, YOU CAN'T HELP ME! GET OUT OF HERE! MAKE YOUR OWN THINGS!!

AND DON'T BOTHER ME ANY MORE! DO YOU HEAR ME?

LITTLE BROTHERS CAN SURE BE A NUISANCE SOMETIMES!

SCHULZ

WHAT'S THE MATTER WITH YOU, SCHROEDER?

THAT'S THE THIRD GROUND BALL YOU'VE MISSED TODAY!

I SUPPOSE YOU'RE GONNA SAY IT TOOK A BAD BOUNCE AGAIN, HUH?!

YES, I AM!!
SCHULZ

WHAT A TEAM! GOOD GRIEF!!

I'VE GOT A CATCHER WHO CAN'T SEE, A FIRST BASEMAN WHO'S ONLY THREE FEET TALL, AND AN OUTFIELDER WHO CAN'T THROW!

CAN'T THROW? I'VE NEVER HEARD OF SUCH A THING...

WELL, NOW YOU HAVE!
SCHULZ

CHARLIE BROWN, I CAN'T PLAY CENTER FIELD ANY MORE..

WHY NOT?
THE **WEEDS** ARE TOO TALL OUT THERE!

OH, GOOD GRIEF STOP COMPLAINING, AND GET GOING!
ALL RIGHT..
SCHULZ

BUT SOMEBODY BETTER TELL ME WHEN THE INNING IS OVER!

!

WHAM

BOY, THERE'S NOTHING LIKE HAVING FOUR FEET!
SCHULZ

I FEEL ON EDGE TODAY..

I FEEL ALL NERVOUS AND TENSE!

PSYCHIATRISTS WILL TELL YOU THAT THERE'S NO BETTER WAY TO RELAX THAN TO LIE WITH YOUR HEAD IN YOUR WATER DISH!
SCHULZ

SCHOOL IS GETTING YOU DOWN, ISN'T IT, CHARLIE BROWN?

WHEN YOU COME HOME IN THE AFTERNOON, YOU NEED SOMETHING TO HELP YOU TO UNWIND...YOU NEED TO RELAX..

I KNOW I DO...

BUT WHO WANTS TO LIE WITH HIS HEAD IN A WATER DISH?!
SCHULZ

SIGH

SCHULZ

SIGH

AND THEY CALL **ME** PECULIAR!
SCHULZ

PEANUTS
Z

TICKLE TICKLE TICKLE

TICKLE TICKLE TICKLE TICKLE
HEE HEE HEE HEE HEE

OH, NOT ON THE FEET! OH, NO! PLEASE! NOT ON THE FEET!!
HEE HEE HEE
TICKLE! TICKLE! TICKLE!

HEE HEE HEE HEE HEE HEE

OH, MAN! I'M EXHAUSTED! OH, MY RIBS! OH, MAN! WHEW

I HAVEN'T LAUGHED SO MUCH IN A YEAR...WHAT A GIRL! WOW!

IT MUST BE NICE TO BE ABLE TO BRING SO MUCH HAPPINESS INTO SOMEONE'S LIFE..
SCHULZ

PEANUTS®
DISGRACEFUL!
OH, GO AWAY!

YOU AND THAT STUPID BLANKET! ARE YOU GONNA CARRY THAT THING AROUND THE REST OF YOUR LIFE?

WHEN ARE YOU GOING TO LEARN TO STAND ON YOUR OWN TWO FEET?
WADDYA MEAN?!

'E GOT JUST AS MUCH WILL POWER AS ANYONE
SE! SEE? I DON'T NEED THIS BLANKET! I CAN
ROW IT AWAY ANYTIME I WANT TO! ANYTIME!

GOOD GRIEF!

YOU'RE A HOPELESS CASE, LINUS...
I THOUGHT I COULD DO IT... I ACTUALLY THOUGHT I COULD DO IT...
SCHULZ

A WOODEN RIFLE WITH A RUBBER BAYONET!! BOY, IS THAT EVER SLICK!

ARGHH!

GEE, I WISH I HAD ONE OF THOSE...

I'M ALWAYS INTRIGUED BY EDUCATIONAL TOYS!
SCHULZ

YOU THINK I DON'T APPRECIATE CLASSICAL MUSIC, DON'T YOU SCHROEDER?

WELL, YOU PLAY SOMETHING FOR ME, AND WE'LL SEE IF I CAN APPRECIATE IT...

I APPRECIATED IT!!
SCHULZ

THIS, LINUS, IS A GIANT OAK!
OAK?!!

WHEN OAK TREES GET REAL OLD, THEY'RE CUT DOWN, AND USED TO MAKE KNOTTY-PINE RECREATION ROOMS
KNOTTY-PINE?!

OH, I CAN'T STAND IT...I JUST CAN'T STAND IT....

LISTENING TO LUCY'S LECTURES ALWAYS MAKES MY STOMACH HURT...
SCHULZ

THIS, LINUS, IS A PALM TREE..
GOOD GRIEF!

IT GETS ITS NAME FROM THE FACT THAT THE AVERAGE PERSON CAN PUT HIS HAND CLEAR AROUND IT..

LUCY! YOU'RE KILLING ME! THESE STUPID THINGS YOU TELL HIM ... THEY GET ME SO WORKED UP, MY STOMACH HURTS!

JUST IGNORE HIM, LINUS..NOW, OVER HERE IS A BAMBOO TREE ...
OW! OW! OW!
SCHULZ

NOW, THIS, LINUS, IS A TELEPHONE POLE...

YOU'LL BE INTERESTED TO KNOW THAT TELEPHONE POLES ARE NOT POLES AT ALL!

THEY'RE REALLY A KIND OF TREE DEVELOPED BY THE PHONE COMPANY SPECIALLY FOR THEIR USE..

OW! OW! OW!
SCHULZ

WHAT DO YOU MEAN, I MAKE YOUR STOMACH HURT?!

YOU DO! YOU SAY STUPID THINGS, AND THEN I GET ALL WORKED UP, AND MY STOMACH STARTS TO HURT!

JUST BECAUSE OF WHAT I SAY CHARLIE BROWN?
YES!

ARE YOU SURE IT ISN'T LOVE?
SCHULZ

LEAVES ARE A FASCINATING STUDY, LINUS..

MOST PEOPLE THINK THAT THE LEAVES JUST FALL OFF WHEN AUTUMN COMES...
MY STOMACH!

BUT THE **TRUTH** IS THAT THEY ALL **JUMP** OFF BEFORE THE **SQUIRRELS** CAN GET 'EM!

THAT DID IT! MOVE OVER, CHARLIE BROWN..
SCHULZ

PRETTY SPEEDY FOR SUCH A LITTLE GUY!
SCHULZ

PEANUTS®

CLOMP!

WHAM!

SECURITY, LIKE LIBERTY, HAS TO BE WON AND REWON MANY TIMES...
BEAT AGAIN!

YOU NITWIT! YOU BIRDBRAIN!
PEANUTS

YOU'RE NOT SO SMART!

YOU BLOCKHEAD! YOU NUMSKULL!

YOU THINK YOU'RE SO SMART! WELL, YOU'RE NOT! YOU'RE STUPID!! DO YOU HEAR ME? YOU'RE STUPID!

CHARLIE BROWN, CAN YOU SEE WHO THAT IS?

NO...THEY'RE TOO FAR AWAY... I CAN'T MAKE OUT WHO IT IS...

I FORGOT WHO I WAS YELLING AT!
SCHULZ

TOSS THAT PENNY IN THE AIR, AND I'LL SHOW YOU SOMETHING..

O.K.... SHOW ME SOMETHING...

BANG!

FASTEST GUN IN THE WEST!
SCHULZ

MY DAD HAS A BETTER UNDERSTANDING OF THE MORAL PROBLEMS CONFRONTING OUR YOUTH OF TODAY THAN YOUR DAD

OH, GOOD GRIEF!
SCHULZ

MY DAD HAS PEACE OF MIND!

I CAN'T STAND IT!
SCHULZ

MY DAD HAS A BETTER JOB THAN YOUR DAD!

MY DAD HAS A BIGGER CAR THAN YOUR DAD!

MY DAD HAS A SON!
SCHULZ

C'MON! HIT ONE OUT HERE!!!

WHAT'S THE MATTER? CAN'T YA HIT 'EM THIS FAR? ARE Y'WEAK, OR SOMETHING ?

WHAT DO Y'THINK I'M STANDIN' OUT HERE FOR, MY HEALTH? C'MON! HIT ONE! WHAT DO...

SCHULZ

I WONDER WHY SOME OF US WERE BORN DOGS WHILE OTHERS WERE BORN PEOPLE...

IS IT JUST PURE CHANCE, OR WHAT IS IT?

SOMEHOW, THE WHOLE THING DOESN'T SEEM VERY FAIR..

WHY SHOULD I HAVE BEEN THE LUCKY ONE?
SCHULZ

EMPTY WATER DISH!
SCHULZ

I WAS JUST TRYING TO TALK WITH THAT LITTLE GIRL UP THE STREET...

BUT I COULDN'T SAY A WORD... I JUST **STOOD** THERE ALL EMBARRASSED AND CONFUSED

I GOT SO SELF-CONSCIOUS I DIDN'T KNOW WHAT TO DO..

SO I **HIT** HER!!
SCHULZ

PEANUTS
by
CHARLES M. SCHULZ

DID YOU GET THAT KITE UP ALL BY YOURSELF, LINUS?
YUP!

DID YOU HAVE ANY TROUBLE?
NOPE!

DIDN'T YOUR KITE GET TANGLED UP IN ANY TREES OR AROUND SOME TELEPHONE WIRES OR EVEN GO DOWN A SEWER?
NOPE!

SIGH

I DIDN'T THINK IT WOULD BE RIGHT TO LET A LITTLE KID LIKE HIM SEE ME CRY..

PEANUTS

SCHROEDER, DO PIANO PLAYERS MAKE A LOT OF MONEY?

MONEY?

WHO CARES ABOUT MONEY?! THIS IS **ART**, YOU BLOCKHEAD!!

THIS IS GREAT MUSIC I'M PLAYING, AND PLAYING GREAT MUSIC IS AN **ART**!! DO YOU HEAR ME? **AN ART!**

ART! ART! ART! ART! ART!
WHAM
WHAM
WHAM
WHAM
WHAM

YOU FASCINATE ME!
SCHULZ

HI, FUZZY-FACE!
"FUZZY-FACE"?!

FUZZY-FACE?!

SIGH I MUST BE GETTING OLD AND SENSITIVE...

A FEW YEARS AGO SOMETHING LIKE THAT NEVER WOULD HAVE BOTHERED ME!
SCHULZ

"FUZZY-FACE"! HE CALLED ME "FUZZY-FACE"..

IT'S WRONG TO BE UPSET BY SUCH A LITTLE THING... I'LL HAVE TO GET HOLD OF MYSELF..

"FUZZY-FACE"! GOOD GRIEF..
SCHULZ

SNOOPY

SCHULZ
"FUZZY-FACE!"
SIGH

FUZZY-FACE! HE WALKED BY, AND HE SAID, " HI, FUZZY-FACE!"
SNIF!

I CAN'T REMEMBER WHEN ANYTHING HAS UPSET ME SO..

STILL...I DON'T KNOW WHY IT SHOULD...

AFTER ALL, WHAT DOES HE EXPECT ME TO BE, **CLEAN-SHAVEN**?
SCHULZ

HERE COMES CHARLIE BROWN.. IF HE CALLS ME "FUZZY-FACE" AGAIN, I DON'T KNOW WHAT I'LL DO!

HI, FUZZY-FACE!!

I WAS RIGHT...I DIDN'T KNOW WHAT TO DO!
SCHULZ

Jane sees Tom. Tom can skip. Jane can skip.

Rex sees Jane and Tom. Rex runs to Jane and Tom.

HOW DO YOU LIKE IT SO FAR?
GREAT! GREAT! DON'T STOP NOW!

I'M GLAD YOU LIKE IT. LATER ON THE SUSPENSE BECOMES ALMOST UNBEARABLE!
SCHULZ

WINTER IS ON ITS WAY, CHARLIE BROWN.

THE DAYS ARE GETTING SHORTER..

IT'S A GOOD THING...

THE WAY MY DAYS HAVE BEEN GOING LATELY, I'D JUST AS SOON HAVE THEM NOT LAST TOO LONG!
SCHULZ

WAS BEETHOVEN EVER A TEEN-AGER?
SCHULZ

PEANUTS
C'MON! HIT ONE OUT HERE!

GREATEST CATCH I'VE EVER SEEN!
SCHULZ

!
PEANUTS
YAWN!

CLOMP!

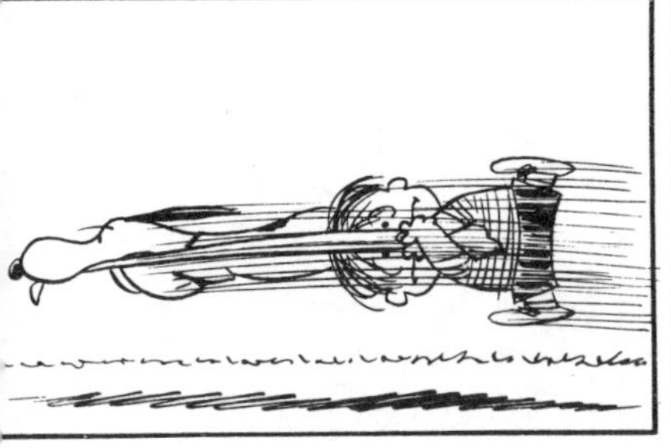

AND **THERE** HE **GOES**!
WHOOSH!

I'M THE FIRST DOG EVER TO LAUNCH A HUMAN BEING!
SCHULZ

WHAT IN THE WORLD ARE **YOU** DOING?

I'M DRAWING IN THE AIR... I CAN DO LANDSCAPES, ABSTRACTIONS AND PORTRAITS..

NOW, WILL YOU KINDLY STEP ASIDE?

YOU'RE STANDING RIGHT IN THE MIDDLE OF AN UNFINISHED PORTRAIT OF ABRAHAM LINCOLN!
SCHULZ

DRAWING IN THE AIR HAS MANY ADVANTAGES..

THE MATERIALS ARE CHEAP, AND YOU HAVE LOTS OF ROOM IN WHICH TO WORK..

YOU CAN DRAW WITH BOLD...

...SWEEPING STROKES!
SCHULZ

LUCY THINKS I'M CRAZY..

BUT FOR CENTURIES CHILDREN HAVE BEEN DRAWING IN THE AIR...

I HAVE MERELY TAKEN AN OLD ART-FORM, AND HAVE GIVEN IT NEW STATURE!

FANTASTIC!
SCHULZ

I FORGOT TO SIGN IT!
SCHULZ

DO YOU LIKE IT?
SCHULZ

DRAWING IN THE AIR IS SO PRACTICAL..

YOU DON'T NEED PENCILS, AND YOU NEVER HAVE TO WORRY ABOUT RUNNING OUT OF PAPER

NOTHING CAN INTERRUPT YOUR WORK...**ABSOLUTELY NOTHING!**

SCHULZ

Z

OH, COME NOW! LET'S NOT GET RIDICULOUS!
SCHULZ

BOY, WHAT A DAY!

EVERYTHING I'VE TRIED TO DO HAS GONE WRONG!

DON'T BE SO DISTURBED, CHARLIE BROWN... WE ALL HAVE OUR BAD DAYS..

LAST YEAR I WAS THE ONLY PERSON I KNOW WHO HAD **THREE HUNDRED AND SIXTY-FIVE** BAD DAYS!
SCHULZ

HEY! WHAT'RE Y'DOING THERE?!!
WHAT'RE Y'DOING WITH THOSE PLIERS?
HEY!

PEANUTS®

THE REASON I CAN GUARANTEE THIS PARACHUTE, CHARLIE BROWN, IS THAT I MADE IT MYSELF..

THIS IS A GOOD HEAVY BLANKET, AND THESE ARE VERY STOUT ROPES..
PUT MY CAP ON FOR ME, WILL YOU?

THERE..NOW, ALL YOU HAVE TO DO IS JUMP OFF THAT STUMP, AND FLOAT GENTLY TO THE GROUND..

JUST WHAT I WAS AFRAID OF.. HE'S GETTING COLD FEET...

GERONIMO!
WUMP!

MMGBMM MGMMBM MMGMM

I THINK I'D BETTER GO HOME AN' SEE WHAT'S ON T.V.
SCHULZ

JUST BECAUSE YOU'RE HAPPY TODAY, DOESN'T MEAN YOU'LL BE HAPPY TOMORROW!

HAPPINESS ISN'T EVERYTHING, YOU KNOW!

IT'LL NEVER BRING YOU PEACE OF MIND!
SCHULZ

DANCE, DANCE, DANCE, DANCE, DANCE!

CAN'T YOU BE SERIOUS EVEN FOR A MOMENT?!

HE HE HE HE HE HE HE
GOOD GRIEF!
SCHULZ

STUPID DOG!
SCHULZ

FLOODS, FIRE AND FAMINE!
?

DOOM, DEFEAT AND DESPAIR!

I GUESS IT'S NO USE.. ⁂ SIGH ⁂

NOTHING SEEMS TO DISTURB HIM!
SCHULZ

YOU'LL BE SORRY, SNOOPY!

MY GREAT-GRANDMOTHER SAYS IF YOU'RE TOO HAPPY TODAY, SOMETHING BAD WILL HAPPEN TO YOU TOMORROW!

ARE YOU TRYING TO MAKE A FOOL OUT OF MY GREAT-GRANDMOTHER?
SCHULZ

?

'IF YOU CAN'T LICK 'EM, JOIN 'EM!'
SCHULZ

ARE YOU TAKING A BATH OR ARE YOU GOING ON VACATION?
SCHULZ

I WONDER IF THERE ARE ANY DOGS ON THE MOON?
SNOOPY

MAYBE THERE ARE...AND MAYBE UP THERE THE DOGS ARE IN CHARGE, AND THE PEOPLE HAVE TO DO WHATEVER THE DOGS SAY..
SNOOPY

I SHOULDN'T THINK ABOUT THINGS LIKE THAT..I GET ALL WORKED UP, AND THEN I CAN'T SLEEP..
SNOOPY
SCHULZ

PEANUTS

LUCY!

LUCY, THERE'S A PORCUPINE IN OUR YARD!

A PORCUPINE? WHAT WAS IT DOING?
NOTHING.. IT WAS JUST LOOKING AT ME..

SEE? IT JUST SITS THERE LOOKING AT ME..

THAT'S NOT A PORCUPINE! THAT'S JUST A **BUSH**!
OH...

GOOD GRIEF!

SCHULZ

STOP LOOKING AT ME!

PEANUTS®

!

"RAIN, RAIN, GO AWAY.. COME AGAIN SOME **OTHER** DAY !!"

I **SAID** "RAIN, RAIN, GO AWAY.. COME AGAIN SOME **OTHER** DAY !!!"

YOU'RE NOT LISTENING!
SCHULZ

ANOTHER FEW WEEKS AND ALL THE BIRDS WILL BE COMING BACK...

COMING BACK? COMING BACK FROM WHERE?
FROM THE SOUTH.. DIDN'T YOU KNOW THAT BIRDS FLY SOUTH FOR THE WINTER?

HA HA HA HA HA HA HA

IN ALL MY LIFE, CHARLIE BROWN, I'VE NEVER KNOWN ANYONE WITH AN IMAGINATION LIKE YOURS!
SCHULZ

I TELL YOU, LUCY, BIRDS **DO** FLY SOUTH DURING THE WINTER!

SURE, THEY DO, CHARLIE BROWN... AND THEY FLY **WEST** DURING THE **SPRING** AND **EAST** DURING THE **FALL**

HA! HA! HA! HA! HA!

I FEEL LIKE GOING HOME TO BED, BUT IT'S ONLY NOON...
SCHULZ

CHICKENS ARE BIRDS AREN'T THEY?

YOU NEVER SEE A CHICKEN FLYING SOUTH FOR THE WINTER, DO YOU?

HAVE YOU EVER SEEN A CHICKEN FLYING SOUTH?

CHICKENS ARE BIRDS, AREN'T THEY?
GOOD GRIEF!!!
SCHULZ

I ASKED MY TEACHER TODAY ABOUT THIS BIRD BUSINESS..
OH?

SHE SAID YOU WERE RIGHT, CHARLIE BROWN... SOME BIRDS DO FLY SOUTH DURING THE WINTER..

YOU KNOW WHAT?
WHAT?

I THINK I'LL SEE IF THEY'LL LET ME CHANGE TEACHERS..
SCHULZ

ANTS FASCINATE ME...

THEY'RE ALWAYS SO BUSY SCURRYING HERE AND THERE...

WHAT ENERGY!

I'D MAKE A LOUSY ANT..
SCHULZ

YOU THINK YOU CAN SAY JUST ANYTHING TO ME, DON'T YOU?

DON'T YOU THINK I HAVE ANY FEELINGS? DON'T YOU THINK I'M LIKE EVERYONE ELSE?

THE TOPS OF YOUR FEET ARE GETTING FAT, CHARLIE BROWN..
SCHULZ

I'LL THROW THE BALL... WHO'LL CHASE IT?

WHO'S GONNA CHASE IT? I'LL THROW IT... WHO'LL CHASE IT?

SIGH

I NEVER VOLUNTEER FOR ANYTHING!
SCHULZ

HMM...

LISTEN TO THIS, CHARLIE BROWN..

"THE HAPPIEST TIME OF LIFE IS BETWEEN THE AGES OF THIRTY AND FIFTY.."

I KNEW I WAS UNHAPPY!!!
SCHULZ

PEANUTS®

YOU'RE SLOWING DOWN, "PIG-PEN."...

WAIT A MINUTE...I THINK THERE'S SOME SAND IN MY SHOES...

THERE...THAT'S BETTER!

I JUST CAN'T RUN IF I HAVE SOMETHING IN MY SHOE...
good grief!
SCHULZ

PEANUTS
THIS IS HOPELESS!

I CAN'T FIND THE BALL!

WADDYA MEAN, PICK IT UP?!

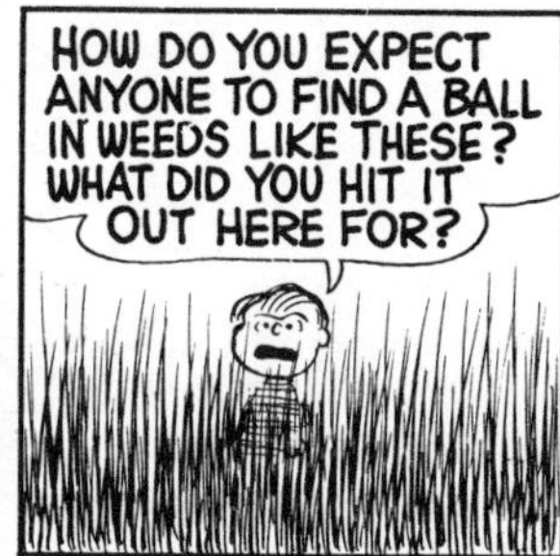
HOW DO YOU EXPECT ANYONE TO FIND A BALL IN WEEDS LIKE THESE? WHAT DID YOU HIT IT OUT HERE FOR?

T'S IMPOSSIBLE! OF COURSE, I'M OOKING! I SAID I CAN'T FIND IT! F I COULD FIND IT, WOULD I STILL BE OUT HERE?

THIS IS HOPELESS! NOBODY COULD FIND ANYTHING OUT HERE! YOU COULDN'T FIND A BATTLESHIP OUT HERE IF IT..

..WAIT A MINUTE...

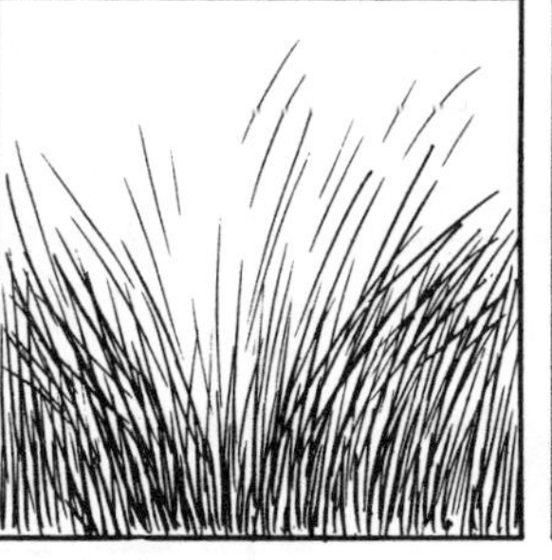

I FOUND IT...
SCHULZ

CLOMP!

DEFT, BOY...DEFT!
SCHULZ

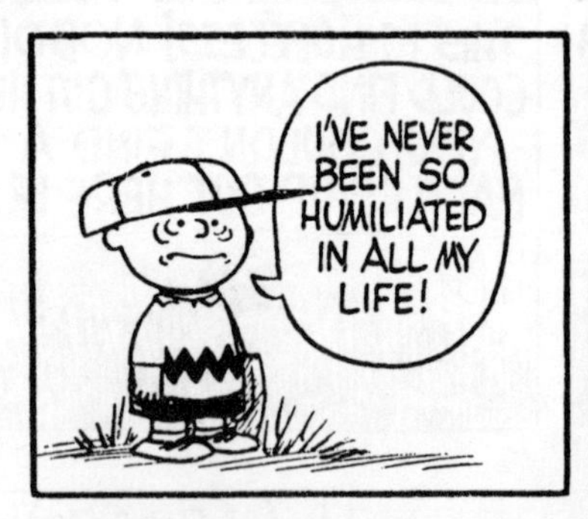
I'VE NEVER BEEN SO HUMILIATED IN ALL MY LIFE!

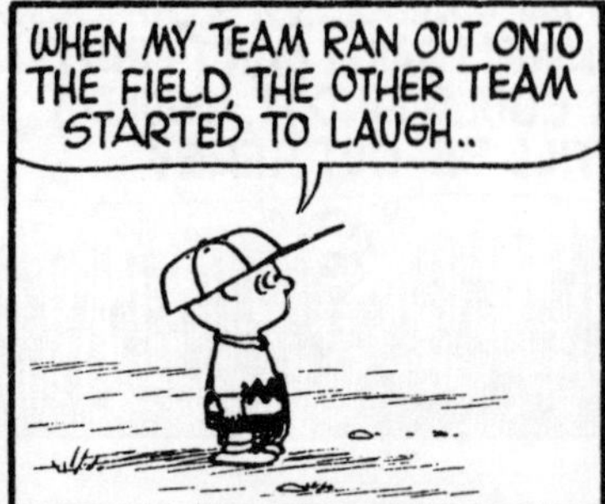
WHEN MY TEAM RAN OUT ONTO THE FIELD, THE OTHER TEAM STARTED TO LAUGH..

THEY LAUGHED AND LAUGHED AND LAUGHED, AND THEN THEY ALL WENT HOME!

RATS!
SCHULZ

THEY WOULDN'T EVEN PLAY US...THEY JUST LAUGHED AT US!

RATS, RATS, RATS, RATS, RATS, RATS, RATS, RATS, RATS, RATS!

RATS!
SCHULZ

DO YOU STILL WANT ME OUT IN CENTER FIELD, CHARLIE BROWN?

NO! DON'T YOU UNDERSTAND?! THEY JUST LAUGHED AT US! THERE'S NOT GOING TO BE ANY GAME!! GO ON HOME!!

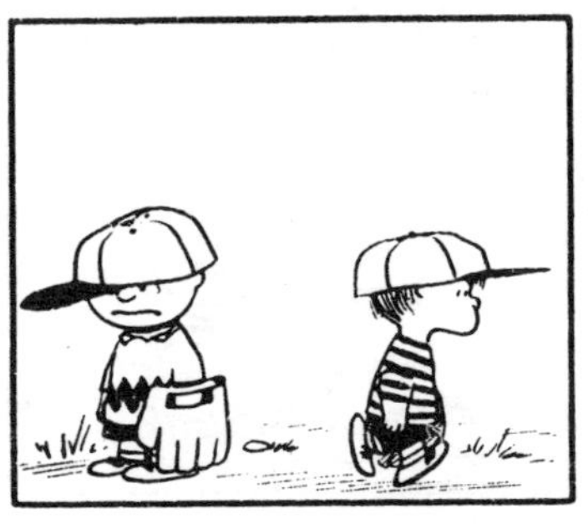

JUST AS A MATTER OF CURIOSITY, WHERE WAS CENTER FIELD?
SCHULZ

"MANAGER"..... HA!!

SCHULZ

YOU KNOW WHAT BOTHERS ME THE MOST?

I FEEL THAT I'VE LET DOWN YOU PLAYERS WHO HAD FAITH IN ME AS YOUR MANAGER..

OH, WELL, IF THAT'S WHAT'S BOTHERING YOU, CHARLIE BROWN, JUST FORGET IT..

WE NEVER REALLY **HAD** ANY FAITH IN YOU!
SCHULZ

SNOOPY

!
SNOOPY

ARF!
SNOOPY

CRAZY SALESMEN!
SNOOPY
SCHULZ

HOW ARE YOU DOING IN SCHOOL THESE DAYS, CHARLIE BROWN?

OH, FAIRLY WELL, I GUESS... I'M HAVING MOST OF MY TROUBLE IN ARITHMETIC..

I SHOULD THINK YOU'D LIKE ARITHMETIC...IT'S A VERY PRECISE SUBJECT..

THAT'S JUST THE TROUBLE. I'M AT MY BEST IN SOMETHING WHERE THE ANSWERS ARE MOSTLY A MATTER OF OPINION!
SCHULZ

PEANUTS
by
CHARLES M. SCHULZ
WHAT ARE YOU WATCHING?
NONE OF YOUR BUSINESS!

I WANNA WATCH MY PROGRAM..

GET OUT OF HERE!

YOU ALWAYS GET TO WATCH YOUR PROGRAMS, AND I NEVE GET TO WATCH MY PROGRAMS

DO YOU WANNA GET HIT?! I'LL SLUG YOU A GOOD ONE!

BROTHER OR NO BROTHER, I'LL RUN ROUGHSHOD OVER YOU

WHAT ARE YOU DOING?
I'M TURNING OFF YOUR PROGRAM, AND TURNING ON MINE..

YOU DON'T FRIGHTEN ME ONE BIT!

WAAH!

PEANUTS

CLOMP!
AAUGH!

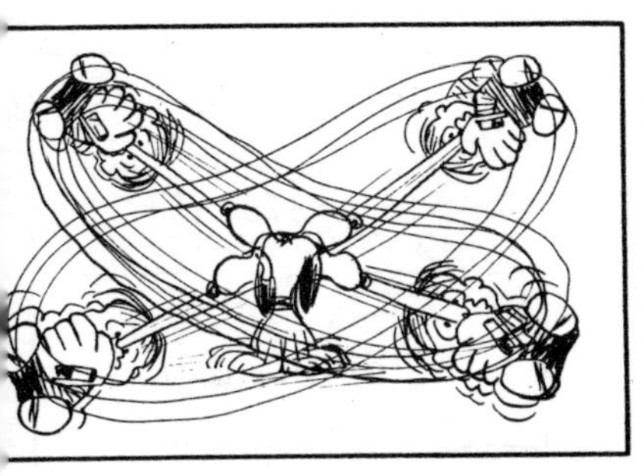

NO MANAGER IN THE HISTORY OF BASEBALL HAS EVER HAD TO GO THROUGH WHAT I HAVE TO GO THROUGH!
SCHULZ

DEAR SANTA.. I AM HAVING A FRIEND OF MINE WRITE THIS LETTER

I AM TOO SMALL TO KNOW HOW TO WRITE...I AM JUST A LITTLE BOY... JUST A HELPLESS LITTLE BOY...

I AM TOO YOUNG TO SET DOWN WITH MY OWN HAND THE WORDS I WOULD LIKE TO WRITE, BUT I HAVE A KIND FRIEND..HE IS TO BE MY PEN..HE IS TO...

IF YOU WANT TO STOP WRITING AND WIPE AWAY A TEAR, YOU MAY!
SCHULZ

OKAY, LINUS. WHAT DO YOU WANT TO SAY NEXT?
WELL, LET'S SEE... HOW ABOUT THIS?

OH, DEAR SANTA, HOW WE HAVE LONGED FOR YOUR RETURN! HOW WE HAVE SEARCHED THE SKIES LOOKING FOR YOUR 'SLEIGH OF HAPPINESS'!

YOU CAN'T SAY THINGS LIKE THAT! DO YOU THINK HE'S GOING TO BELIEVE YOU?

HE HAS TO BELIEVE ME.. THAT'S HIS JOB!
SCHULZ

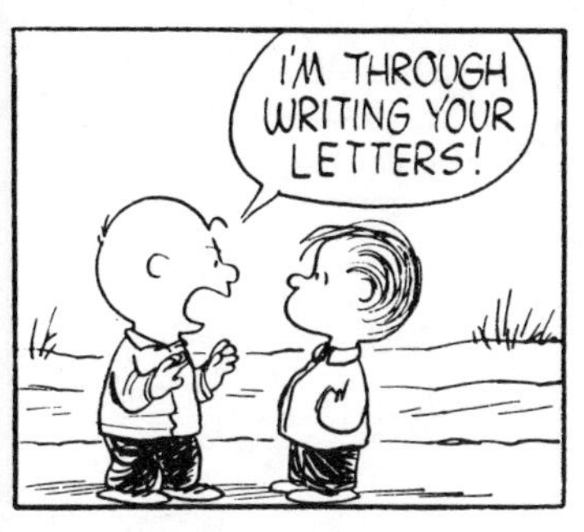
I'M THROUGH WRITING YOUR LETTERS!

YOU SAY ALL THESE FANCY THINGS TO SANTA CLAUS, BUT YOU DON'T **MEAN** THEM! YOU'RE A **HYPOCRITE**!

A **HYPOCRITE**? HOW CAN I BE A HYPOCRITE?

I HAVEN'T EVEN REACHED THE AGE OF ACCOUNTABILITY!!
SCHULZ

FAREWELL, DEAR SANTA!

HAVE A NICE TRIP HOME!! THANKS FOR COMING! SEE YOU NEXT YEAR!!

WE'LL MISS YOU, DEAR SANTA YOU'LL BE IN OUR EVERY THOUGHT, OUR EVERY DREAM!

I'D BETTER GO HOME..I FEEL A SUDDEN WAVE OF NAUSEA!
SCHULZ

WELL, JUST REMEMBER THAT **YOUR** KIND LIVE OFF **MY** KIND! **WE** MAY FLATTER SANTA CLAUS, BUT **YOU** GET YOUR SHARE OF THE PRESENTS!

SCHROEDER, WHAT IF YOU AND I WERE A COUPLE OF MARRIED ESKIMOS?

AND WHAT IF YOU WANTED TO BRING A GRAND PIANO INTO OUR IGLOO, AND WHAT IF I SAID THERE WASN'T ROOM, AND..

SCHULZ
SIGH

THAT KID IN SCHOOL SURE SAID SOME MEAN THINGS ABOUT YOU TODAY..

HOW COME YOU DIDN'T HIT HIM?

I HAVE OBSERVED THAT WHENEVER YOU TRY TO HIT SOMEBODY THERE IS A TENDENCY FOR THEM TO TRY TO HIT YOU BACK

YOU ARE A SHREWD JUDGE OF HUMAN NATURE, CHARLIE BROWN
SCHULZ

PEANUTS®
WELL!

LOOK, SCHROEDER..THEY PRINTED MY LETTER IN THE PAPER..

"DEAR AGNES, I AM IN LOVE WITH A BOY WHO DOESN'T EVEN KNOW I AM ALIV

"ALL HE EVER SEEMS TO THINK OF IS HIS STUPID PIANO AND THAT STUPID OL' BEETHOVEN!"

"CAN YOU GIVE ME ANY ADVICE?"

KLUNK!

AND HERE'S HER ANSWER..."DEAR LUCY,....NEVER FALL IN LOVE WITH A MUSICIAN." HMMM... I KIND OF SUSPECTED THAT...
SCHULZ

PEANUTS®

"..AND THIS PIECE WAS DEDICATED BY BEETHOVEN TO HER MAJESTY, THE EMPRESS."

HOW COME YOU'VE NEVER DONE THAT FOR ME, SCHROEDER?

THERE! I DEDICATE THAT TO YOU!
SCHULZ

"BOYS ARE ROTTEN FILLED WITH COTTON.."

"GIRLS ARE DANDY FILLED WITH CANDY!"

GENERALITIES!!
SCHULZ

AND TWO MORE MAKE THIRTY-SIX..

I'VE COUNTED THIRTY-SIX ELECTRICAL OUTLETS IN OUR HOME

WHAT WE **REALLY** NEED ARE SOME **EMOTIONAL** OUTLETS!
SCHULZ

I NEVER REALIZED THAT THE WORLD BELONGS TO WHOEVER HAS THE BIGGEST TEETH!
SCHULZ

THAT'S PRETTY GOOD...

BUT I DON'T THINK IT'S GOOD ENOUGH..

THEY GOT THIRTY-TWO IN...

YEAH, BUT JUST REMEMBER... A TELEPHONE BOOTH IS A LOT BIGGER!
SCHULZ

WELL, SNOOPY, HOW ARE YOU TODAY?

WHAT DO THINK OF THE WORLD IN GENERAL? WHAT DO YOU THINK ABOUT LIFE?

WHAT DO YOU THINK ABOUT TAXES, THEOLOGY, TADPOLES, TAMALES, TIME-TABLES, TEA AND TENNESSEE ERNIE?

HE'S GOT THE RIGHT IDEA... IF YOU'RE NOT SURE, JUST DON'T SAY ANYTHING..
SCHULZ

WOULDN'T IT BE WONDERFUL IF THERE WERE NO HATRED?

WOULDN'T IT BE WONDERFUL IF THERE WERE NO HATRED IN THE WHOLE WORLD?
4-2

WHY DOES THIS INTEREST YOU SO MUCH, CHARLIE BROWN?

THEN NOBODY WOULD HATE **ME**!
SCHULZ

HAYDN'S "SURPRISE" SYMPHONY..
SCHULZ

PHOOEY!
PEANUTS

I FEEL MEAN TODAY!

WHEN I FEEL MEAN, NOBODY BETTER GET IN MY WAY!

NOBODY!
SCHULZ

PEANUTS

I BEG YOUR PARDON...
?

THANK YOU, GIRLS..
SCHULZ

WELL?! WHO'S GOING TO OPEN THE DOOR?!
SCHULZ

LOOK AT ME.. I'M A **GIANT**!

YOU SURE DON'T **LOOK** LIKE A GIANT...

GIANTS HAVE BIG BOOTS, AND THEY DON'T WEAR SUIT COATS

I'M AN **INDUSTRIAL** GIANT!
SCHULZ

THEY SAY KIDS DON'T HAVE THE IMAGINATION THAT THEY USED TO HAVE..

THEY SAY THAT ALL WE DO NOWADAYS IS SIT AROUND, AND WATCH TELEVISION...

IS THAT RIGHT?

SCHULZ
RIDICULOUS!

YOU KNOW WHAT ELSE THEY SAY IS WRONG WITH OUR GENERATION, CHARLIE BROWN?

THEY SAY WE DON'T KNOW HOW TO CREATE OUR OWN FUN THESE DAYS... THEY SAY WE DON'T KNOW HOW TO BUILD THINGS..

THEY SAY WE HAVE TOO MANY TOYS ALREADY MADE FOR US..

SCHULZ
THAT'S **OUTRAGEOUS**!

MY DAD SAYS THAT KIDS THESE DAYS HAVE TOO MUCH MONEY

EXCUSE ME, CHARLIE BROWN..DO YOU HAVE CHANGE FOR A TEN?

SURE...HERE YOU ARE.. NINE ONES AND FOUR QUARTERS...OKAY?
FINE... THANK YOU..

NONSENSE! YOUR DAD DOESN'T KNOW WHAT HE'S TALKING ABOUT!
SCHULZ

YOU KNOW WHAT MY GRANDFATHER SAYS?

HE SAYS THAT KIDS THESE DAYS NEED MORE OF THE OL' RAZOR STROP!

MAYBE HE'S RIGHT..

HAVE YOU EVER BEEN HIT WITH AN ELECTRIC RAZOR?
SCHULZ

MY GRANDFATHER SAYS THAT IN **HIS** DAY, KIDS DIDN'T GET INTO SO MUCH MISCHIEF..

HE SAYS THEY WERE TOO BUSY MAKING THINGS WITH THEIR OWN HANDS..

OH? WHAT SORT OF THINGS?

SLINGSHOTS!
SCHULZ

MY GRANDFATHER SAYS THAT IN HIS DAY KIDS DIDN'T DRAG BLANKETS AROUND..

YOUR GRANDFATHER DIDN'T HAVE TO WORRY ABOUT BEING RUN DOWN IN THE STREET BY BLOCKHEADS!

HE DIDN'T HAVE TO WORRY ABOUT BEING BOMBED FROM OUTER SPACE!!!

HE DIDN'T HAVE TO WORRY ABOUT..
GOOD GRIEF!
SCHULZ

PEANUTS®

PEANUTS®

WHOP!

YER OUT!

YOU AND THAT STUPID BLANKET!
SCHULZ

FROM NOW ON, WHEN I SPEAK, YOU COME CRAWLING!

ALL RIGHT, SNOOPY... COME!!

SCHULZ

YOU'RE GETTING TO BE A REAL SMART ALECK!

YOU'RE GETTING TO BE..

SMACK!

SCHULZ

BOY, IF THAT DOESN'T TAKE THE CAKE!

WHAT'S THE MATTER, LUCY?
THAT GIRL IN THE NEXT BLOCK..

SHE GOT MAD JUST BECAUSE I HIT HER BROTHER...

I WOULDN'T GET MAD IF SHE HIT MY BROTHER!
SCHULZ

THE MAN I MARRY MUST BE TALL AND HANDSOME..

THE MAN I MARRY MUST BE STRONG AND BRAVE AND TRUE..

THE MAN I MARRY MUST KNOW HOW TO PLAY THE ACCORDION..

GOOD!

HAVE YOU EVER HEARD OF THE "BEAT GENERATION", CHARLIE BROWN?

OH, YES...

I'M A CHARTER MEMBER!
SCHULZ

LICK
LICK
LICK

SLURP!

LICK
LICK
LICK

WE DOGS ARE SO HUMBLE!
SCHULZ

"PIG-PEN," WHY ARE YOU ALWAYS SO DIRTY?

WHEN IN THE WORLD ARE YOU GOING TO CLEAN UP?

I HAVE AFFIXED TO ME THE DIRT AND DUST OF COUNTLESS AGES..

WHO AM I TO DISTURB HISTORY?
SCHULZ

?
?
CLICK
CLICK
CLICK
CLICK
CLICK
CLICK

?
CLICK
CLICK
CLICK
CLICK
CLICK

CLICK CLICK
CLICK CLICK
CLICK

TOENAILS!
SCHULZ

PEANUTS®

THERE!

I HAVE A SURPRISE FOR YOU, SCHROEDER..

WHAT IS IT?
A PICTURE OF BEETHOVEN! I DREW IT MYSELF

WELL, I'LL BE!! THIS IS SWELL!
I THOUGHT MAYBE YOU'D LIKE TO HAVE IT TO HANG IN YOUR ROOM..

THAT'S A GOOD IDEA..
I'M SO HAPPY THA
YOU LIKE IT, SCHROED
I WOULD HAVE BEE
SO DISAPPOINT
IF YOU HADN'T

NOW, WHERE DO YOU THINK I SHOULD HANG IT?
!

HANG IT AROUND YOUR NECK, YOU BLOCKHEAD!